CARING

by Jane Belk Moncure
illustrated by Helen Endres

Distributed by
Standard Publishing,
Cincinnati, Ohio 45231.

THE
CHILD'S
WORLD

ELGIN, ILLINOIS 60120

To the teacher or parent:

One of the main principles of the Christian faith is that we be concerned, caring people. As parents and teachers, we begin early to communicate this truth to our children—both by our actions and our teachings. This book is an attempt to help in that task.

It does not attempt to present all the Biblical teachings on caring, but it does introduce the Bible truth that God cares for us and that He wants us to be caring people. It then seeks to help children understand how they can carry out the Bible truth.

Most children have been involved in situations similar to those presented in this book and will be happy to talk about them.

Use the book to introduce discussion or to make practical application of Bible stories that deal with caring.

Distributed by Standard Publishing, 8121 Hamilton Avenue, Cincinnati, Ohio 45231.

Library of Congress Cataloging in Publication Data

Moncure, Jane Belk.
    Caring.

    (What does the Bible say?)
    1. Sympathy—Juvenile literature. 2. Empathy—Juvenile literature. I. Endres, Helen. II. Title.
III. Series.
BV4647.S9M66   241'.4   80-14200
ISBN 0-89565-166-1

CARING

The Bible says:

"He careth for you."
        –1 *Peter* 5:7

God cares for each of us. God wants
us to be caring people. What is caring?

When I hold my little brother on my shoulders so he can pick apples too, that's caring.

When I help a turtle across a path
in the park so he will be safe, that's
caring.

Caring is feeding the wild birds—
not just when it snows, but all winter
long!

Caring is picking up paper and trash
someone else left under the picnic table.

When a friend asks for another push in the swing, and it's the tenth push and you do it anyway, that's caring.

When you leave wild flowers to
bloom along a mountain trail so others
can enjoy them too, that's caring.

When you put your bicycle in the garage so it won't get wet or stolen, that's caring.

Caring is teaching a friend how to turn
a cartwheel.

Caring is wrapping your coat around a
friend on a chilly day.

When you make up your bed,

put your clothes away,

and keep your toys picked up, without
being asked again and again, that's
caring.

Caring is helping Dad plant a new tree
after a storm knocked down the old one.

When you get a bandage for a friend
who scraped her knee, that's caring.

When you feed and brush your puppy
and give him clean water every day,
that's caring.

When you faithfully pick up your
bowl and glass and spoon, and carry
them to the sink, that's caring.

Caring is being a friend to a new
person in the neighborhood.

Believe it or not, caring is listening to your parents and trying to do the things they ask you to do. They ask because they care.

God cares for you.

God cares for me. I thank Him for His care.

Tell me, how do you show caring?

About the Author:

Jane Belk Moncure, author of many books and stories for young children, is a graduate of Virginia Commonwealth University and Columbia University. She has taught nursery, kindergarten and primary children in Europe and America. Mrs. Moncure has taught early childhood education while serving on the faculties of Virginia Commonwealth University and the University of Richmond. She was the first president of the Virginia Association for Early Childhood Education and has been recognized widely for her services to young children. She is married to Dr. James A. Moncure, Vice President of Elon College, and currently lives in Burlington, North Carolina. Mrs. Moncure is the daughter of a minister and has been deeply involved in Christian work all her life.

About the Artist:

Helen Endres is a commercial artist, designer and illustrator of children's books. She has lived and worked in the Chicago area since coming from her native Oklahoma in 1952. Graduated from Tulsa University with a BA, she received further training at Hallmark in Kansas City and from the Chicago Art Institute. Ms. Endres attributes much of her creative achievement to the advice and encouragement of her Chicago contemporaries and to the good humor and patience of the hundreds of young models who have posed for her.